Fast Facts about Texas

Location: In the southwestern United States
Area: 266,807 square miles (693,698 square kilometers)
Population: 16,986,510
Capital: Austin
Date admitted to the Union: December 29, 1845; the 28th state
Largest cities: Houston, Dallas, San Antonio, El Paso, Austin, Fort Worth, Arlington, Corpus Christi, Lubbock, Garland
Nickname: The Lone Star State
State bird: Mockingbird
State flower: Bluebonnet
State reptile: Horned lizard
State tree: Pecan
State song: "Texas, Our Texas" by Gladys Yoakum Wright and William J. Marsh

The Rio Grande forms the border between Texas and Mexico.

Chapter 1

Music in Texas

Country music is big in Texas. In fact, it is popular all over the country. Cowboys and cowgirls everywhere are putting on hats, boots, and jeans to dance to country hits.

They are doing line dances. They dance the cotton-eyed Joe. They swing to the Texas two-step. It all started in Texas and the south.

Country music has always been popular in Texas. Many famous country musicians were born there. Gene Autry, Clint Black, Waylon Jennings, George Jones, Willie Nelson, Buck

Dancing to country music is popular in Texas and throughout the United States.

Owens, George Strait, and Tanya Tucker are all from Texas. There are country-music radio stations throughout the state.

Texans like other kinds of music, too. Blues singers traveled from town to town in the early 20th century. They played at parties and at small clubs.

Some Texas **jazz** musicians used the blues sound. They put it in their own music. Texas rock 'n roll stars like Buddy Holly and Janis Joplin added the blues sound, too.

A Big Place

Texas is a big state. It was the largest state in the Union until Alaska became a state in 1959. Alaska is the only state bigger than Texas.

Texas has 305,951 miles (489,522 kilometers) of roads. This is the longest road system in the United States.

Texas was an independent nation before it became a state. It has been the home of three

Texans fought Mexicans at the Alamo during the Texas Revolution. The old mission still stands in San Antonio.

U.S. presidents. They are Dwight Eisenhower, Lyndon Johnson, and George Bush.

Texans are proud of their state and its history. They call their state the Lone Star State. The future is bright for Texas.

Chapter 2
The Land

Because Texas is so big, it has many different types of land. Some of the land is forest. Some of it is mountains. Plains and deserts cover thousands of square miles.

West Texas

West Texas is hot and dry. Very little rain falls on the high plains, deserts, and mountains. There are few towns. Lonely roads stretch across the land. Rattlesnakes, coyotes, and bighorn sheep live in the region.

A flat-topped mesa rises above the desert of West Texas.

The Guadalupe Mountains are in West Texas. They are steep and rocky. Guadalupe Peak is near the border with New Mexico. It is 8,751 feet (2,625 meters) high. It is the highest point in Texas.

The Rio Grande forms the border between Texas and Mexico. The largest city in West Texas is El Paso. It is across the Rio Grande from the Mexican city of Juárez.

Central Texas

Plains spread across central and northern Texas. They take up more land than many U.S. states.

There are many cattle **ranches.** They have vast fields and pastures. Herds of **longhorn cattle** graze on the land.

The largest ranch in the United States is in north-central Texas. It is the Waggoner Ranch. It covers more than 800 square miles (2,080 square kilometers).

A longhorn steer grazes on the high plains of Texas.

The Panhandle

Northwest Texas is called the **Panhandle**. The land is flat. There are few trees. Strong, cold winds blow there in the winter. Sometimes it snows. The Panhandle has thunderstorms and tornadoes in the spring and summer.

Amarillo is the largest city in the Panhandle. Palo Duro Canyon State Park is south of Amarillo. It has steep cliffs of layered rock.

East Texas

East Texas is covered with pine forests. The land is hilly. There are many small rivers. The **fertile** soil helps farmers grow rice, cotton, and vegetables.

The Sabine River forms the border with Louisiana. Across the Red River to the north is Oklahoma. The clay on the river bottom is a brownish-red color.

This is the rainiest part of the state. Summers in East Texas are hot, humid, and sometimes stormy.

The Gulf Coast

Texas has a long coast on the Gulf of Mexico. The land is flat and sandy. Some alligators still live in the wetlands behind the Gulf beaches.

Padre Island is a narrow strip of soft sand. It runs along the coast across from Corpus

A fisherman and a heron share a beach on the Gulf of Mexico.

Christi. It goes south all the way to the Rio Grande and Mexico.

Hurricanes sometimes strike the Gulf coast. A hurricane hit Galveston in 1900. There was no protection from the ocean waves. The storm killed more than 5,000 people. It was the worst **natural disaster** ever in the United States.

TREES
REDOAK
LIVEOAK
VINE
RIPENED
HILL
COUNTRY
1015
ONION

Chapter 3

The People

There are nearly 17 million people living in Texas. Only New York and California have more residents.

The strong Texas economy still attracts **immigrants**. About 4 percent of the population was born in a foreign country.

Europeans

Seventy-five percent of Texans have European roots. Many are descended from German, English, or Polish immigrants. These immigrants began arriving in the early 19th century.

Many people with German roots live in a town called New Braunfels. It is in central Texas, near San Antonio.

A roadside vendor sells onions, tomatoes, pecans, and other produce grown in Texas.

Workers prepare meat in an old-fashioned butcher shop.

Czech-speaking settlers moved into the surrounding plains. Texas also has many people with Scotch-Irish **ancestors.**

There are some small Cajun communities in southeastern Texas. Cajuns are French-speaking people. Their ancestors moved to the southern U.S. from Canada in the 18th century. Most Cajuns live across the Texas border in Louisiana.

Hispanic Americans

One out of every four Texans is Hispanic. They speak Spanish or have Spanish-speaking ancestors. Some Hispanics are descended from Mexican farmers. The farmers lived in Texas when it was a part of Mexico. San Antonio was founded by Mexicans in the early 18th century.

South Texas has a large Hispanic population. The people have kept many Mexican traditions. Brownsville is on the Mexican border. Every year, Hispanic Americans there celebrate Charro Days with music, dancing, and rodeos.

African Americans

African Americans make up about 12 percent of the population. Some of their ancestors were slaves who worked on plantations in Texas. Many former slaves became sharecroppers after the Civil War

(1861-1865). They paid rent for their homes with crops they harvested. Some African-American men became cowboys on trail drives.

Many African Americans celebrate Juneteenth every year. It marks the day, June 19, 1863, that Texas slaves learned about the Emancipation Proclamation. President Abraham Lincoln issued the proclamation that freed the southern slaves on January 1, 1863, during the Civil War.

Asian Americans

Asian immigrants have come to Texas in recent times. They have come from Cambodia, Korea, and the Philippines.

Many Vietnamese people came to Texas in 1974 during the Vietnam War (1954-1975). Many of the Vietnamese immigrants worked as shrimpers in the Gulf of Mexico.

Native Americans

Texas has a small population of Native Americans. Most Indians were forced to move

A crowd watches the Dallas Cowboys prepare for another National Football League season.

out of the state in the 19th century. Many moved north to Oklahoma.

Texas has three Indian reservations. The Kickapoo, Alabama-Coushatta, and Tiwa Indians live on these lands. The reservations cover about 5,000 acres (2,000 hectares) of land.

Chapter 4

Texas History

Native Americans were the first people to live in Texas. Apache and Kiowa hunters lived in the mountains and on the plains. The Caddos included several different tribes. *Tejas* was a Caddo word meaning friend. Settlers turned the word Tejas into Texas.

Spanish Missions

The first European explorer to reach Texas was Alonso Álvarez de Piñeda. He sailed past

Stephen F. Austin helped build the first U.S. settlement in Texas. He brought 300 families with him.

the mouth of the Rio Grande in 1519. Spanish explorers claimed the land for Spain but did not settle there.

In 1682, Spanish priests built a mission at El Paso. Later, farmers from Mexico began settling north of the Rio Grande. They brought herds of longhorn cattle with them.

Spanish priests built more missions. Forts called presidios were built close to many of the missions. The presidios protected the missions from Indian attacks. A mission opened at San Antonio de Valero in 1718. Later, it was called the Alamo.

The Comanche and Kiowa Indians did not want people on their hunting grounds. They raided settlements and attacked missions. The raids drove many settlers out of Texas.

Settlers from the United States arrived in 1821. Stephen F. Austin brought 300 families with him. They farmed along the Brazos River. That same year, Mexico won independence from Spain.

The Comanche were forced out of Texas. Their camps at Palo Duro Canyon were destroyed in 1874.

Revolt Against Mexico

Most Texans did not want to be a part of Mexico. A war broke out in 1835. The Mexican army was led by General Antonio Lopez de Santa Anna. The army attacked the Alamo in February 1836. Only 189 Texans were protecting the Alamo. Davy Crockett, Jim Bowie, and others fought to the death against more than 4,000 Mexican troops.

The defenders of the Alamo fought to the death against the Mexican army. Mexico later lost the Texas Revolution.

Texas fighters defeated the Mexican troops at the Battle of San Jacinto on April 21, 1836. The Texans shouted “Remember the Alamo!” as they fought. Texas had won its independence from Mexico. It was now an independent country called the Republic of Texas. Sam

Houston was the first president of the new republic.

Statehood

Texas became a state on December 29, 1845. The next year, war broke out between the United States and Mexico. The United States won the war in 1848. The Rio Grande became the border between Texas and Mexico.

Texas had been admitted to the Union as a slave state. The conflict over slavery and states' rights led to the Civil War in 1861. Texas and 10 other southern states seceded from the Union. They formed the Confederacy.

In 1865, the South surrendered and the war ended. The last battle of the Civil War was at Palmito Hill in Texas. It took place after the surrender. The news of the North's victory had not yet reached Texas.

Cattle Drives and Oil Drilling

Many Texans established huge cattle ranches after the war. Cowboys drove the cattle north to markets in the Midwest.

Almost 50,000 barrels of oil spouted every day from an early gusher at Beaumont, Texas.

The cattle drives ended in the 1880s. New railroads were built across the plains. Ranchers began moving their cattle by train.

The Texas economy changed in the 1890s. **Wildcatters** came to the state to drill for oil. The oil industry grew quickly.

War and Depression

The demand for oil was high during World War I (1914-1918). This drove up the price. Texas companies sold oil to the rest of the country. The oil industry and oil workers made a lot of money.

The Great Depression (1929-1939) wrecked the nation's economy. The demand for oil dropped. Many oil workers lost their jobs. Many left for other states.

World War II (1939-1945) helped the Texas economy. New companies built ships, airplanes, and weapons for the war. Texas became an important manufacturing state.

High-Tech Texas

Houston became the location of the Manned Spacecraft Center in the 1960s. Workers at the center directed space missions. They directed the first mission to the moon in 1969.

Since the 1960s, Texas has become the home of many high-tech companies. Today, Texas can survive a drop in oil prices because it has a more diverse economy. The state's economy is one of the strongest in the United States.

Chapter 5
Texas Business

For many years, Texas depended on the oil industry. The state did well when the price of oil was high. It suffered when oil prices dropped.

Today, Texas has many different industries. This makes it easier to handle changes in oil prices.

Manufacturing

There are thousands of manufacturing companies in Texas. Chemical plants make rubber, plastic, and fertilizers. Food processing plants prepare vegetables, fish, and fruits. The food is shipped around the country.

A powerful drill cuts stone at a Texas quarry.

High-tech companies make computers and electronic parts. There are many such companies near Austin. Texas Instruments is one of the biggest high-tech companies in the world.

Agriculture

More cattle are raised in Texas than in any other state. Texas farmers also raise sheep, goats, and horses.

Farms in the Panhandle grow wheat, sorghum, and corn. Texas produces more than 4 million bales of cotton every year.

Fruit trees are common in the Rio Grande Valley. There are groves of grapefruit, oranges, and nut trees.

Mining and Energy

Texas mines produce sulfur, coal, salt, and gypsum. Texas has supplies of limestone, sand, and gravel. Drilling teams search for underground oil and natural gas.

Oil-drilling is still a big business in Texas. Only four countries produce more oil than Texas.

Semitrailer trucks carry goods across the wide open spaces of Texas.

Huge drilling platforms sit in the Gulf of Mexico. Pipelines carry the oil to refineries along the coast. These refineries turn the oil into gasoline.

Service Businesses

Seventy percent of Texas workers are employed in service areas. They work at banks or insurance companies. They teach or work in hospitals. They work in hotels or restaurants or stores. Service areas cover many kinds of jobs.

Chapter 6
Seeing the Sights

Texas has many different landscapes. There are forests, canyons, seacoasts, and mountains to explore. Old forts and historic towns give visitors a look at the state's rich history.

There is something to do in every season. Rodeos and roundups are common in the fall. In the winter, bird lovers can watch thousands of migrating birds along the Gulf Coast. San Antonio holds a fiesta every spring. Water sports are popular on the lakes and rivers during the hot summers.

The homes of army officers still stand at the Fort Davis National Historic Site in southwestern Texas.

There are many small towns in Texas.

West Texas

West Texas is the hottest part of Texas. It is also the most mountainous. Big Bend National Park is named for a sharp bend in the Rio Grande. Hiking trails in the park lead up mountains. The trails cross steep canyons. Visitors can spot bighorn sheep, wild deer, and antelope in the rocky hills.

The city of El Paso lies on the banks of the Rio Grande. Most of its residents are Hispanic. The Mexican city of Juárez is across the river. Fort Bliss is a huge military base north of El Paso.

Vast plains cover West Texas, too. Cattle and sheep graze on the ranges. Pumps bring oil up from the ground. Midland and Odessa are two important oil towns.

Central Texas

The Colorado River flows through central Texas. San Angelo and the capital of Austin are on the river. The Alamo still stands in downtown San Antonio. The city also has River Walk. This is an area of shops and restaurants along the San Antonio River.

The Lyndon Baines Johnson National Historical Park is at Johnson City. This was the home of the late President Lyndon Johnson.

East Texas

Much of East Texas is covered with pine forests. Dams on the rivers have created many artificial lakes. They are called reservoirs. One of these is Lake Texoma, on the Red River. It is the largest lake in Texas.

Dallas and Fort Worth are two large cities in northeastern Texas. Every October, the Texas State Fair takes place in Dallas. It is the biggest state fair in the country. President John F. Kennedy was assassinated in Dallas on November 22, 1963. A museum and memorial plaza honor the president.

The Amon Carter Museum is in Fort Worth. The museum has a collection of western paintings and sculpture.

The Big Thicket Preserve is a dark, mysterious forest near the town of Kountze. Swamps and marshes surround the trees. Most people explore the Big Thicket in boats and canoes.

The Gulf Coast

Every winter, tourists from the northern U.S. visit the warm Gulf Coast. Padre Island National Seashore lies just off the coast. It is a long strip of sandy land. The island is 100 miles (160 kilometers) long.

Mission San Jose is in San Antonio. It is a reminder of the time Texas belonged to Spain and Mexico.

Corpus Christi is across from Padre Island. This is the deepest port on the Gulf. Across Corpus Christi Bay is Mustang Island. At one time, the island was home to a herd of wild horses.

Galveston is an important port. It lies on a small island in the Gulf. Old warehouses, commercial buildings, and homes there have been restored. A trolley called the Galveston

A rugged rock formation rises in the Guadalupe Mountains.

Flyer runs through town. Several fishing piers reach out into the Gulf.

Houston is the largest city in Texas. It has many skyscrapers and is the center of the oil industry.

The Johnson Space Center is just south of Houston. At Mission Control, visitors can watch engineers direct space flights. Moon rocks, space suits, and rockets are on display.

Texas Timeline

About 8,000 B.C.—Ancestors of the Native Americans begin settling in Texas.

1519—Alonso Álvarez de Piñeda explores the Rio Grande River.

1682—First Spanish mission built near El Paso.

1731—Town of San Antonio founded.

1821—Mexico wins independence from Spain.

1822—American settlers establish farms along the Brazos River.

1835—War breaks out between Americans and Mexicans in Texas.

1845—Texas becomes the 28th state.

1866—Cattle drives begin along the trails heading north.

1880s—Texas ranchers use new railroads to send their cattle to market.

1894—Water drillers strike oil at Corsicana, near Dallas.

The site of a 19th-century Texas farm is marked by the ruins of an old stone house.

1901—Wildcatters strike oil at Spindletop Hill.

1918—Texas gives women the right to vote.

1925—Miriam "Ma" Ferguson becomes first woman governor of Texas.

1963—Assassination of President John F. Kennedy in Dallas.

1969—Manned Spacecraft Center in Houston directs mission to the moon.

1993—Standoff in Waco between federal agents and members of the Branch Davidian religious cult ends in death and destruction.

Famous Texans

Alvin Ailey (1931-1989) A dancer and choreographer who founded the Alvin Ailey American Dance Theater; born in Rogers.

George Bush (1924-) Forty-first president of the United States; lives in Texas.

Henry Cisneros (1947-) Former mayor of San Antonio; first Hispanic mayor of a major U.S. city; born in San Antonio.

Dwight Eisenhower (1890-1969) Supreme commander of Allied forces during World War II; 34th president of the United States; born in Denison.

Oveta Culp Hobby (1905-1995) Appointed country's first secretary of health, education, and welfare in 1953; born in Killeen.

Lyndon Baines Johnson (1908-1973) Thirty-sixth president of the United States; born near Johnson City.

Barbara Jordan (1936-1996) First southern black woman to be elected to the U.S. Congress; born in Houston.

Willie Nelson (1933-) Singer who created "outlaw" country music; born in Abbott.

Quanah Parker (c.1845-1911) Comanche chief who encouraged his people to settle as farmers and attend school but not forget their Indian heritage; born near Lubbock.

Katherine Anne Porter (1890-1980) Novelist and short-story writer who won the Pulitzer Prize in 1966; born in Indian Creek.

Ann Richards (1933-)Prominent politician; elected state's second woman governor in 1990; born near Waco.

Nolan Ryan (1947-) Retired major league baseball pitcher; holds the record for most no-hitters (seven) and most strikeouts in a single season (383 in 1973); born in Refugio.

Lee Trevino (1939-) Professional golfer; first won the U.S. Open in 1968; born in Dallas.

Mildred "Babe" Didrikson Zaharias (1914-1956) Olympic track and field champion and golf star; known as the greatest woman athlete in first half of 20th century; born in Port Arthur.

Glossary

ancestor—a person from whom one is descended, such as a grandmother or a great-grandfather

fertile—favorable to the growth of plants and crops

immigrant—a person who comes to another country to settle

jazz—improvised music originated by African Americans in the late 19th century

longhorn cattle—breed of cattle with long, spreading horns raised in the Southwest

natural disaster—destruction caused by such natural occurrences as tornadoes, hurricanes, earthquakes, volcanoes, and blizzards

Panhandle—a strip of land in northwest Texas that looks like the handle of a pan

ranch—large farm in western North America on which cattle, horses, or sheep are raised

wildcatters—people who drill for oil in areas not known to have oil

To Learn More

Fradin, Dennis Brindell. *Texas.* From Sea to Shining Sea. Chicago: Children's Press, 1992.

Fritz, Jean. *Make Way for Sam Houston.* New York: Putnam, 1986.

Pelta, Kathy. *Texas.* Minneapolis: Lerner Publications, 1994.

Stein, R. Conrad. *Texas.* America the Beautiful. Chicago: Children's Press, 1989.

Useful Addresses

Johnson Space Center
2101 NASA Road 1
Houston, TX 77058

National Cowgirl Hall of Fame
515 Avenue B
Hereford, TX 79045

Sea World
10500 Sea World Drive
San Antonio, TX 78251

Texas Ranger Hall of Fame Museum
Box 2570
Waco, TX 76702

Index